REGIONS OF THE WORLD

Africa South of the Sahara

Rob Bowden

Heinemann Library
Chicago, Illinois

Customer Service 888-454-2279
Visit our Web site at www.heinemannraintree.
com

Editorial: Andrew Farrow
Design: Steve Mead and Q2A Creative
Illustrations: International Mapping
    Associates, Inc
Picture Research: Melissa Allison
Production: Alison Parsons

Originated by Chroma Graphics (Overseas) Pte. Ltd
Printed and Bound in the United States of
America, North Mankato, MN.

14 13 12
10 9 8 7 6 5 4

ISBNs: 978-1-4034-9901-1 (hardcover)
        978-1-4034-9910-3 (paperback)

**Library of Congress Cataloging-in-Publication
Data**

Bowden, Rob, 1973-
   Africa south of the Sahara / Rob Bowden.
     . p. cm. -- (Regions of the world)
   Includes bibliographical references and index.
   ISBN 978-1-4034-9901-1 (hc) -- ISBN 978-1-4034-
9910-3 (pb)
   1. Africa, Sub-Saharan--Juvenile literature. I.
Title.
   DT351.B68 2007
   967--dc22
                                       2007011623

092012
006906RP

Acknowledgments
The publishers would like to thank the following
for permission to reproduce photographs:

© Corbis pp. 48 (Ed Kashi), 44 (Gideon Mendel), 27
(Gideon Mendel/ActionAid), 31 top (Hervé Collart),
16, 24, 28 (Liba Taylor), 31 lower (Louise Gubb), 11
(Nic Bothma), 34 (Patrick Robert), 33 (Paul Almasy),
51 (Reuters/STR); © EASI-Images pp. 21 (Ed Parker), 35
(Jenny Matthews), 38 (Rob Bowden), 12, 29, 36, 52 (Roy
Maconachie); © Getty Images pp. 18 (Photonica), 15
(Reportage), 4, 46 (Stone); PA Photos pp. 55 (AP), 40
(AP/Khalil Senosi), 53 (AP/Sayyid Azim); © Photolibrary
pp. 22 (Alan & Sandy Carey), 49 (Nick Gordon), 19
(OSF); © Robert Harding p. 43 (L Taylor); © Still Pictures
p. 41 (Friedrich Stark); © UPPA p. 47 (World Pictures)

Cover photograph of schoolchildren in Burkina Faso
reproduced with permission of Still Pictures/Ron
Gilling.

Every effort has been made to contact copyright
holders of any material reproduced in this book.
Any omissions will be rectified in subsequent
printings if notice is given to the publishers.

Contents

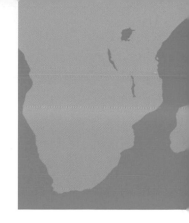

Any words appearing in the text in bold, **like this**, are explained in the Glossary.

Introducing Africa South of the Sahara

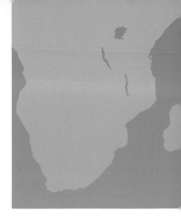

The Sahara Desert in Africa is the world's largest desert. At more than 3.3 million square miles (8.6 million square kilometers), it is larger than Australia or all of Western Europe! This enormous desert forms a divide that stretches from east to west across the African **continent**. The countries to the north of this divide are known as North Africa. The people of North Africa are mainly Arabic, and Islam is the main religion. North Africa shares similar cultures and languages with the Middle East, and with it forms a region known as North Africa and the Middle East. The countries to the south of the Sahara form a region known as Africa south of the Sahara, or sub-Saharan Africa. This stretches from the southern edge of the Sahara Desert, in the north, to the southern tip of Africa at Cape Agulhas in South Africa.

The countries of sub-Saharan Africa share many things in common. By world standards they are mostly poor, and nearly all have fast-growing populations. But sub-Saharan Africa is also a region of great variety. From languages to wildlife, economies to landscapes, and cultures to resources, each country is different.

← People gather to trade and exchange news at a rural market in Burundi. Markets such as this form the center of community life across much of sub-Saharan Africa.

The countries of sub-Saharan Africa

Africa south of the Sahara is made up of 49 countries. They range in size from Mayotte at just 144 square miles (374 square kilometers) to Sudan, which covers 967,499 square miles (2,505,810 square kilometers). Together, sub-Saharan Africa covers an area of 9,493,590 square miles (24,588,285 square kilometers). This is an area larger than the United States, Australia and New Zealand, Western Europe, India, and Japan combined!

A region of regions

Africa south of the Sahara is such a large area, with so many countries, that it is often divided into four smaller regions.

Regions of sub-Saharan Africa

Region	Countries
West Africa	Sao Tome and Principe, Nigeria, Niger, Benin, Togo, Ghana, Burkina Faso, Cote d'Ivoire, Liberia, Sierra Leone, Guinea, Guinea Bissau, Senegal, The Gambia, Mauritania, Mali, Cape Verde
Central Africa	Angola, Democratic Republic of Congo, Congo, Central African Republic, Gabon, Equatorial Guinea, Cameroon, Chad
East Africa	Rwanda, Burundi, Uganda, Kenya, Tanzania, Ethiopia, Somalia, Sudan, Eritrea, Djibouti, Seychelles
Southern Africa	South Africa, Namibia, Botswana, Lesotho, Swaziland, Zimbabwe, Zambia, Mozambique, Malawi, Madagascar, Comoros, Mauritius, Mayotte

The people of sub-Saharan Africa

In 2006, sub-Saharan Africa was home to roughly 768 million people. That is about 12 percent of the world total, and more than the populations of the United States and the European Union combined. The population of sub-Saharan Africa is very unevenly distributed. Just six countries (Nigeria, Ethiopia, Democratic Republic of the Congo, Tanzania, Sudan, and Kenya) have half of the region's population. Nigeria is by far the most populated country, with 134.4 million people in 2006. In contrast, Djibouti, Cape Verde, and Equatorial Guinea have some of the lowest populations, with roughly 500,000 people each.

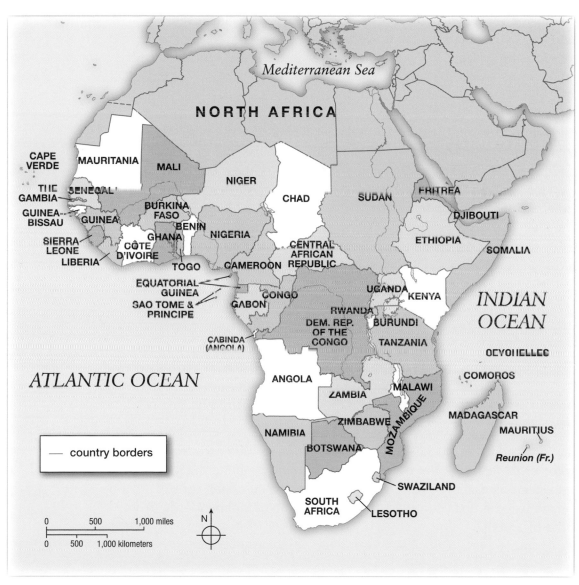

This political map of Africa south of the Sahara shows the 49 countries of the region. All the countries and their statistics are listed on page 56.

Ancient origins

Archaeologists believe that the first humans came from sub-Saharan Africa roughly 100,000 years ago, and gradually spread out across the rest of the world. Our pre-human ancestors also came from sub-Saharan Africa. Evidence found in Tanzania, Kenya, and Ethiopia shows that they had learned to walk upright, build shelters, and cook as long as 1.5 million years ago. Some remains are more than 3 million years old, and this supports the idea that all human life can be traced back to sub-Saharan Africa. For this reason the area is sometimes known as "the cradle of humankind."

Colonialism

Each country in sub-Saharan Africa has its own history, but nearly all share one thing in common—they were once **colonies** of European countries that ruled them. Beginning in the 18th century, European explorers and Christian **missionaries** returned from Africa with reports of gold, diamonds, and exotic spices. This started a scramble for Africa, with the main European powers of the time rushing to conquer and control parts of the region. By 1900, sub-Saharan Africa had been divided up among England, France, Belgium, Portugal, Spain, and Germany.

During the colonial period, the European powers exploited the resources and people of the region for their own benefit. Gold, copper, diamonds, and other minerals were exported back to Europe, and the best farmland was taken over by European settlers. Local people were forced to work for the European landowners, growing export crops such as cotton, tea, coffee, and cocoa. Some European nations even traded in people. They captured them, packed them into ships, and sold them as slaves to work in America or Europe.

During World War II (1939–45), European countries used men from their colonies to help fight the war. When the war was over and the men returned home, they began to demand an end to European control. Ghana was the first country in the region to gain its independence (from Britain), in 1957.

In some countries there was a struggle for independence, as the Europeans tried to hold on to power. In Kenya, for example, a local movement called the Mau Mau attacked European farmers in the hope of driving them off the land. The last country in the region to become independent from Europe was Rhodesia, which became Zimbabwe in 1980.

MOROCCO
TUNISIA
Mediterranean Sea
ALGERIA
LIBYA
EGYPT
FRENCH WEST AFRICA
GAMBIA
PORT. GUINEA
TOGO
NIGERIA
FRENCH EQUATORIAL AFRICA
ANGLO-EGYPTIAN SUDAN
ERITREA
FR.
BRITISH SOMALILAND
SIERRA LEONE
GOLD COAST
ETHIOPIA
LIBERIA
FERNANDO PO
RIO MUNI
KAMERUN
ITALIAN
SÃO TOMÉ
UGANDA
BRITISH EAST AFRICA
INDIAN OCEAN
BELGIAN CONGO
CABINDA
GERMAN EAST AFRICA
Zanzibar
ATLANTIC OCEAN
ANGOLA
N. RHODESIA
NYASALAND
Comoro Is.
GERMAN SOUTHWEST AFRICA
S. RHODESIA
MOZAMBIQUE
MADAGASCAR
WALVIS BAY
BECHUANALAND
SWAZILAND
UNION OF SOUTH AFRICA
BASUTOLAND

Belgian
British
French
German
Italian
Portuguese
Spanish
Independent

0   500   1,000 miles
0   500   1,000 kilometers
N

This map shows sub-Saharan Africa at the time of the peak of colonial power in the region, in 1914.

THE COLONIAL LEGACY

The colonial period made a lasting impact on sub-Saharan Africa. The borders created by the Europeans were not based on existing cultural groupings. Often they divided communities of the same ethnic and language group and threw others, who had once been enemies, together. Lands were also divided: much of the best land is still owned by Europeans and by the local leaders who took over at independence. This has left many poorer families without enough land to support themselves. The region's economy is also still heavily dependent on exporting crops and raw materials for its income. The colonial rulers did not develop skilled industries here, since they would have competed with those industries in Europe.

A poor region

Africa south of the Sahara is the world's poorest region. To put this in perspective, the total economy of the region in 2005 was four times smaller than that of the United Kingdom, and over 23 times smaller than that of the United States. By far the region's wealthiest country is South Africa, which was worth $224.1 billion in 2005. The next wealthiest country is Nigeria, at roughly $75 billion in 2005.

The true poverty of sub-Saharan Africa is better explained by looking at average income. In 2005, this was less than $2,000 per person per year in sub-Saharan Africa. The world average was $9,420, and in the United States and the European Union this was closer to $30,000. Using average incomes as a measure, the World Bank has said that 22 of the 25 poorest nations in the world are in sub-Saharan Africa. The poorest of them all is Burundi in East Africa, at just $640 per person per year.

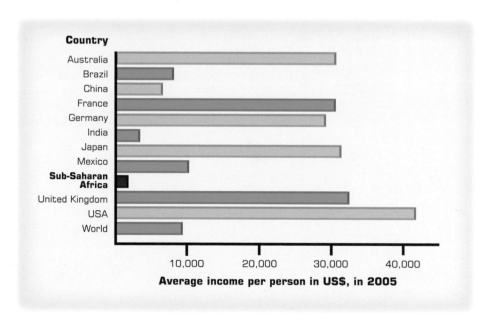

This bar chart shows the poverty of sub-Saharan Africa in comparison to other parts of the world.

Left behind

The severe poverty of sub-Saharan Africa has had a major impact on other areas of life, such as health and education. This is because governments are too poor to invest properly in schools and hospitals, and many people cannot afford to pay for these services themselves. **Life expectancy** today is as low as 35 years in Zambia and Botswana, for example. In addition, millions of young people across the region do not go to school. Of those that do, many will struggle to complete even their primary education. These poor living conditions show that sub-Saharan Africa is a region that has been left behind by the rest of the world.

Challenges ahead

There are new threats to the region, too. A major infectious virus called **HIV** (human immunodeficiency virus) is leading to millions of deaths in sub-Saharan Africa, and millions more are extremely sick. People infected with HIV can eventually suffer from Acquired Immuno-Deficiency Syndrome (**AIDS**), for which there is no cure. There are drugs to help people with HIV/AIDS to live longer, but these are too expensive for most countries to afford.

Another problem in several parts of the region is political instability. This is where governments are weak, or different groups of people are competing to control a country. Sierra Leone, Somalia, Sudan, and the Democratic Republic of the Congo are some of the countries where there have been recent problems. When a country suffers from political instability, it makes it even harder to provide health and education services for the people. It can also damage the economy, making poverty much worse.

↑ This child is a victim of the recent famine in Darfur, Sudan—one example of the impact of conflict and instability, and ongoing poverty, on the people of sub-Saharan Africa.

Natural Features

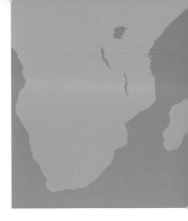

Africa south of the Sahara boasts some of the world's most spectacular landscapes. In the north, the region is dominated by the Sahara Desert, the largest desert in the world. Further south and in Central Africa, tropical forests dominate the landscape. The Congo **rain forest** is the second largest in the world, behind the Amazon rain forest of South America. It covers an area of roughly 888,000 square miles (2.3 million square kilometers), which is about four times the size of France. The main landscape feature in East Africa is the Great Rift Valley, a giant fault line in the Earth's surface that crosses Africa like an enormous scar. East Africa is also home to Lake Victoria, the largest of Africa's lakes and the second largest freshwater lake in the world. Lake Victoria is one source of the River Nile, the longest river in the world. Another of sub-Saharan Africa's great rivers is the Zambezi, which cascades over the world's widest waterfall, Victoria Falls, on the border between Zambia and Zimbabwe.

In addition to the region's spectacular features, the landscapes and **climates** of sub-Saharan Africa provide its people with mixed fortunes. Those living around Lake Victoria, for example, enjoy a fertile land with regular rainfall that is almost perfect for farming. Just a few hundred miles north, however, drought is common and the soils are poor. There are many who struggle to survive in such environments.

← This tree nursery near Kano in northern Nigeria is growing seedlings that will be planted in an effort to combat the widespread problem of desertification (see page 17).

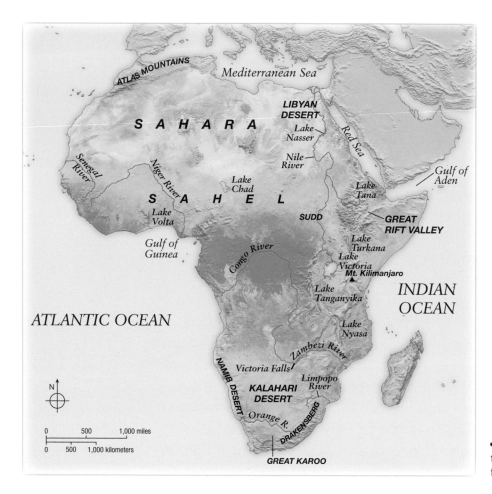

ATLAS MOUNTAINS
Mediterranean Sea
LIBYAN DESERT
S A H A R A
Lake Nasser
Red Sea
Nile River
Senegal River
Niger River
Gulf of Aden
S A H E L
Lake Chad
Lake Tana
Lake Volta
SUDD
GREAT RIFT VALLEY
Gulf of Guinea
Congo River
Lake Turkana
Lake Victoria
Mt. Kilimanjaro
INDIAN OCEAN
Lake Tanganyika
ATLANTIC OCEAN
Lake Nyasa
Zambezi River
Victoria Falls
NAMIB DESERT
KALAHARI DESERT
Limpopo River
N
Orange R.
DRAKENSBERG
0   500   1,000 miles
0   500   1,000 kilometers
GREAT KAROO

← This map shows the key physical features of the region.

The tropics

Almost all of Africa south of the Sahara lies within a region known as the **tropics**. This is a geographical region of Earth that extends for approximately 1,600 miles (2,575 kilometers) on either side of the Equator. The climate of the tropics is generally warmer and wetter than elsewhere in the world, and it varies less through the year. Over such an enormous area, however, the climate of sub-Saharan Africa still varies considerably.

Temperatures across much of sub-Saharan Africa are relatively stable, with only the southern tip of the region experiencing large seasonal changes. Cape Town, for example, varies from a daily average of 53.6 °F (12 °C) in July to 69.8 °F (21 °C) in January. By contrast Mombassa, close to the Equator, has an annual average range of between 76.1 °F (24.5 °C) and 82.4 °F (28 °C).

CLIMATE CHANGE

Most scientists now agree that human actions are changing the world's climate, through the emission of carbon dioxide and other gases into the atmosphere. Sub-Saharan Africa has recently experienced some of its hottest and driest years, but also some extreme rainfall and flooding. These may be the first signs of climate change that would bring new challenges to sub-Saharan Africa. In Uganda and Kenya, a warmer climate might reduce, or even destroy, the valuable tea and coffee crops. In South Africa and elsewhere, water is already desperately scarce and this is expected to become a severe problem. Niger, Chad, Sudan, and Ethiopia will see more frequent droughts due to lower rainfall. Climate change will have other consequences, too. Diseases such as malaria, which is carried by mosquitoes, will spread into regions that were previously too cold for mosquitoes to survive.

Rainfall

Rainfall is the more important variable in sub-Saharan Africa. The rains move as a band from north to south across the region. Their arrival and duration is difficult to predict, and it can cause great suffering if there is either too much or too little. The northern and southern extremes of the region experience the greatest uncertainty. Countries such as Sudan and Niger in the north, and Zimbabwe and Malawi in the south, have suffered major droughts in years when the rains have failed to come.

In Zanzibar, Tanzania, the rains have arrived at last. Zanzibar, like much of the region, is heavily dependent on seasonal rains.

Deserts and drylands

Roughly 47 percent of sub-Saharan Africa comprises **deserts** and **drylands**. These are also known as **arid** regions. Here the average rainfall is less than 20 inches (500 millimeters) per year. Deserts are the driest regions, and the deserts with less than 1 inch (25 millimeters) of rainfall per year are classified as hyper-arid, which means they are extremely dry. The great deserts of sub-Saharan Africa are the Sahara and the Somali deserts in the north of the region, and the Namib and the Kalahari deserts in the southwest. Hyper-arid deserts support very little life, but even here some life manages to survive. In the Namib Desert, for example, the Welwitschia plant (*Welwitschia mirabilis*) survives by collecting moisture from the air. Some Welwitschia are believed to be more than 2,000 years old.

These camels and goats are being led through the desert to water in Darfur, Sudan. The animals are essential to the people's livelihood.

Bordering the deserts are the arid zones. Rainfall here is 1–8 inches (25–200 millimeters) per year. Survival remains difficult, but not impossible. **Nomadic pastoralists** live here, and survive by moving their cattle, goats, sheep, or camels to wherever there are fresh supplies of water and pasture. Arid lands are too dry to grow crops. Semi-arid zones have an annual average rainfall of 8–20 inches (200–500 millimeters). They are more suited to life, though there is a high level of risk as the rains often fail here. Pastoralists also live here, and some drought-resistant crops can be grown. The use of **irrigation** to supplement natural rainfall can help to make farming more reliable.

Desertification

One of the major challenges facing sub-Saharan Africa is **desertification**. This is where land becomes unsuitable for farming or pasture because it becomes more desert-like. A change in the climate, such as a long period of hotter, drier weather, can lead to desertification, but humans are often the major cause. Poor land management, such as over grazing livestock or cutting down trees for fuel, leaves the soil vulnerable to **erosion** by the sun, rain, and wind. Every year millions of tons of soil are eroded in this way. Desertification makes soils less suitable for farming, and can force people to abandon their land. It is estimated that up to 75 percent of sub-Saharan Africa's arid and semi-arid regions are at risk from desertification. Together these are home to roughly 400 million people.

International organizations and governments are working together to try to reduce desertification. One of the most effective measures is to plant trees, which hold the soil together and protect it from the sun and wind. Trees can also provide food for people and animals, and fuel for cooking or construction. Where trees have been planted, desertification has been reduced. Nevertheless, population growth and the pressure on land for farming and other uses mean that desertification remains a major environmental threat.

DRY, BUT NOT ALWAYS

The Sahara Desert is among the driest places on Earth today, but this was not always the case. Evidence such as early cave paintings and fossilized animal remains reveal that it was once much wetter. Roughly 10,000 years ago, parts of the Sahara were home to hippopotamus, giraffe, and elephant. Rock paintings also suggest that early humans were growing crops and raising cattle there. Some say this shows that desertification is only an unavoidable and natural process.

Great rivers

The region includes the sources of four of the world's longest rivers: the Nile, the Congo, the Niger, and the Zambezi. All these rivers and their **basins** (the area of land that feeds water into them) are shared by more than one country (see table below). These countries must cooperate over the management of the river to agree, for example, on the amount of water they can take from it. The rivers provide water for drinking and for irrigation. They are also used for fishing, transportation, and energy production. The Nile, for example, has the Nalubaale (Owen Falls) **hydroelectric power** (HEP) dam at Jinja, in Uganda. This provides almost all of Uganda's electricity, and is soon to be joined by a second dam further downstream. A giant HEP project planned for the Congo would be the biggest in the world, and produce enough electricity to meet all of Africa's current needs.

The Zambezi river cascades into a gorge at Victoria Falls on the border between Zimbabwe and Zambia.

Major rivers of sub-Saharan Africa

River	Length in miles (km)	Countries sharing the river basin
Nile	4,144 (6,670)	Burundi, Rwanda, Uganda, Tanzania, Kenya, Democratic Republic of the Congo, Eritrea, Ethiopia, Sudan, Egypt
Congo	2,920 (4,700)	Democratic Republic of the Congo, Congo, Central African Republic, Angola, Zambia, Tanzania, Cameroon, Burundi, Rwanda, Gabon
Niger	2,598 (4,181)	Nigeria, Mali, Niger, Algeria, Guinea, Cameroon, Burkina Faso, Benin, Ivory Coast, Chad, Sierra Leone
Zambezi	2,200 (3,540)	Zambia, Angola, Zimbabwe, Mozambique, Malawi, Tanzania, Botswana, Namibia, Democratic Republic of the Congo

Lakes

Lake Victoria is the region's largest lake, covering 26,563 square miles (68,800 square kilometers) across Kenya, Tanzania, and Uganda. It is also the source of the White Nile, which exits the lake at Jinja in Uganda on its long journey to Egypt. Thousands of people are involved in both local and commercial fishing here. An estimated 30 million people depend on Lake Victoria for their livelihoods.

Other major lakes in the region include Lake Tanganyika and Lake Malawi. Lake Malawi, in the Great Rift Valley, provides fish for the people of Malawi and Mozambique. Lake Tanganyika is less than half the size of Lake Victoria, but it actually holds more water because it is very deep.

← Lake Nakuru is a soda lake in the Great Rift Valley. These are lakes where volcanic activity and high rates of evaporation have left the water very **alkaline**. Little survives in this water, but it is ideal for flamingos who feed on the algae that thrive there.

Coasts

Many of the region's largest cities are located along its coastline, including Lagos in Nigeria, Cape Town in South Africa, and Dar es Salaam in Tanzania. They developed as natural ports for ships to shelter and trade. Africa's coasts also provide rich fishing grounds that support the local populations. The nations with the largest marine fish catches are South Africa, Namibia, Angola, Nigeria, Mauritania, and Egypt. In recent decades the fishing grounds off West Africa have been fished by commercial fleets from Europe, too. This has led to some concerns that the number of fish is falling.

Mangrove swamps are a form of tropical forest that grow in shallow coastal waters. They are important breeding grounds for many fish species, and protect coastal areas from ocean storms. Many have been destroyed by clearance for building, or by pollution from industry and farming. In Kenya and West Africa, governments and community groups are now taking action to protect the mangroves.

Forests

It is difficult to accurately measure how much of an area is covered by forest, and so figures vary greatly. Some of the best estimates show that in sub-Saharan Africa forests cover roughly 20 percent of the total land area. In the Democratic Republic of the Congo, Congo, Gabon, Cameroon, Angola, Equatorial Guinea, and Guinea Bissau more than 50 percent of the land is forested. These are some of the countries that share the giant Congo rain forest. By contrast, forests cover less than 5 percent of the land area in Lesotho, Mauritania, Niger, Ethiopia, and Burundi. As well as differences in forest area, forest type also varies across the region.

Tropical rain forests

Tropical rain forests dominate around the Equator. These grow in areas of high rainfall and steady temperatures, and grow densely and rapidly. They are home to an enormous variety of species, including the great apes such as the gorilla and chimpanzee. Tropical rain forests also have the most prized trees, whose wood is extremely valuable if sold for export. Other trees are used for local purposes, and foods are also gathered from the forests. This has brought people and wildlife into conflict, so that some species, such as the mountain gorilla, are now extremely endangered.

Dryland forests

Farther from the Equator are the dryland forests. These are made up of shorter, hardy trees that are better able to withstand long periods without rain. The acacia, which has many different types, is one of the most common dryland trees.

Dryland forests are much thinner than tropical rain forests and have fewer species, but they are still important **ecosystems**. They often border areas of grassland (see page 22), and form an important habitat for wildlife including elephant, rhinoceros, giraffe, and leopard.

Humans also use dryland forests for fuel, food, and building materials. Large areas of dryland forest have been destroyed or damaged through clearance for agriculture or settlements. Tree planting is helping to restore some of these areas, but population growth and continuing demands on forest resources mean that only one tree is planted for every 28 that are cut down.

SUSTAINABLE FORESTRY IN THE CONGO

In May 2006, a logging operation in Kabo in the Republic of Congo became the first in the Congo rain forest to be given approval by the Forestry Stewardship Council (FSC). The FSC monitors forestry activities to make sure they are sustainable and protect the local environment, people, and wildlife. The Kabo operation covers an area of 730,000 acres (296,000 hectares), which is home to an estimated 600 forest people. It is also home to many threatened species, including gorilla and elephant. The logging operation there will have to work closely with local people to make sure their lives are not disrupted. For example, the forest people are being helped to create a map showing their hunting grounds and other areas of importance. The logging company will use this map to ensure they plan their harvests around local needs. The company must also advise the local community before it begins any logging.

Kabo is only the second logging operation in tropical Africa to be awarded the FSC certificate. It is hoped that by showing that this logging operation can be both successful and environmentally friendly, more companies will copy the plan. This would help to improve the state of forestry in sub-Saharan Africa, before more of its forests are damaged beyond repair.

 This is the Congo forestry program in Kabo.

Grassland environments

Sub-Saharan Africa has more grassland than any other region of the world, covering roughly 5.6 million square miles (14.5 million square kilometers). This is roughly one and a half times the size of the United States. These grasslands are best known for their remarkable wildlife. The **savanna** plains of the Maasai Mara in Kenya and the Serengeti in Tanzania have the greatest gathering of large mammals anywhere on the planet. Wildebeest, zebra, and antelope live here in the millions, providing a plentiful food source for **predators,** such as lions, leopards, and cheetahs.

These impala are grazing on the plains of the Maasai Mara in Kenya.

Pastoralists

It is not just wildlife that depends on the grasslands, however. They are also important to pastoralists, who raise animals—usually cattle, sheep, and goats—as their main source of food and income. They live throughout the grasslands of sub-Saharan Africa, and have a specialist knowledge of this environment and the seasonal rains that bring fresh pasture for their animals.

Some of the better known pastoral groups in sub-Saharan Africa include the Samburu, Maasai, Hausa, Fulani, Turkana, Tuareg, Dinka, and Himba. Some pastoralists spend many days or weeks away from home, taking their livestock to the best pastures that may be hundreds of miles away. They travel in small groups, with few possessions. When they find water and grazing they make a temporary camp using locally available materials. Some pastoralists, known as nomadic pastoralists, have no permanent home. They are always on the move with their livestock, following seasonal routes and living in temporary shelters.

Pressures on the grasslands

The grasslands of sub-Saharan Africa are under enormous pressure from human activities. Some areas have been protected, as national parks or reserves, but elsewhere there is serious damage and wildlife numbers are falling.

Causes of pressure on grasslands

Cause	Impact on grasslands
Population growth of people and livestock	Greater pressure on grasslands and more competition for pasture. This can lead to fighting between pastoral communities. Less time for the grasslands to recover and increased soil erosion, as livestock overgraze the vegetation.
Farming	Large areas converted to farmland for subsistence or commercial farming. This disrupts traditional pastoral grazing lands and can bring wildlife and people into conflict (wildlife destroying crops, for example).
Fuelwood	Grasslands are often mixed with small areas of forest, or have trees scattered throughout them. Clearing these trees for fuel, especially on the edge of large cities, such as Addis Ababa in Ethiopia, destroys the grassland.
Urbanization	Grasslands are being destroyed by expanding urban centers for building, fuel, brickmaking, timber, food production, and other uses. Increasing water use in cities is also draining water from some grasslands, leading to shortages for pastoralists.
Climate change	Global warming appears to be changing weather patterns in the region, making many grasslands drier. This has an impact on wildlife and livestock. Predictions show that the grasslands could become even drier in the future, some could even become deserts. People and wildlife would have to move if this happened.

LIVING WITH WILDLIFE

The growing population has brought people into greater conflict with the wildlife, as they compete for land and resources. Conflict has also been caused by the creation of some national parks, because they keep pastoralists from using land they have used for many centuries. In Zimbabwe, a project called CAMPFIRE was set up to encourage local people to work with, instead of against, wildlife. Today they see wildlife as a resource, and have set up tourist facilities to earn money from visitors to the wildlife on their lands. Similar projects have been set up in Kenya with the Maasai and Samburu pastoralists. These projects are building new models for people to live with wildlife, helping them to earn money while at the same time protecting the wildlife and grasslands.

People

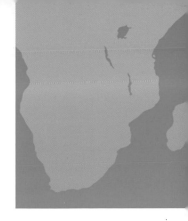

In global terms, sub-Saharan Africa is not heavily populated. In 2006, it had an average **population density** of roughly 12 people per square mile (31 per square kilometer). This is roughly the same as in the United States and Europe, and compares with a world average of 18.5 per square mile (48 per square kilometer). Within the region, East and West Africa have roughly twice the population density of Central and Southern Africa. The most important factor in the population of sub-Saharan Africa is its rapid growth. This region has the fastest growing population in the world, with average growth rates for the period 2000-2005 of more than 3.5 percent per year in Burundi and Uganda. The average for the region as a whole is roughly 2.2 percent per year, which is twice the world average.

The population of sub-Saharan Africa is expected to more than double by 2050, from 768 million in 2006 to roughly 1.692 billion. This would increase its share of world population from just under 12 percent to nearly 19 percent. Some countries will see their population more than double. Uganda, for example, is expected to increase from 30 million people in 2006 to 127 million by 2050.

The people of Africa south of the Sahara are incredibly diverse. They speak hundreds of different languages, and have a range of distinctive cultures. This diversity was not respected when European powers divided Africa into their colonies. As a result, people of very different backgrounds found themselves forced to live together within the new boundaries. In some cases this has led to ongoing tensions between different groups, and even localized conflict.

← These young children are from Burundi. Like many countries in sub-Saharan Africa, Burundi has a very young population, so it is likely to continue growing for many years to come.

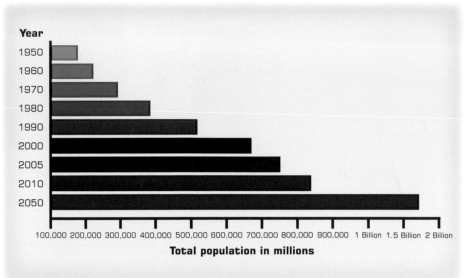

This graph shows the rapid increase in the population of the region over the past 50 years, and the projection of continued increase.

High fertility

Fertility rates measure the number of children a woman is expected to give birth to during her lifetime. In 2006, the average global fertility rate was 2.58, but in sub-Saharan Africa it was just under 5. In parts of the region it was over 6, and in Niger in West Africa it was 7.64. This is the main reason for the region's rapid population growth. People have traditionally had more children in sub-Saharan Africa because many of them would die in childhood. Roughly 15 percent of the region's children still die before their fifth birthday today, compared to roughly 6 percent in Asia and 1 percent or less in North America and Europe. This is, however, much lower than in the past, and is another key factor in the region's growing population. Improvements in healthcare, from **immunization** to simple measures of hygiene, are saving lives by reducing the spread of germs and disease.

A young population

The population of sub-Saharan Africa is very young, with an average life expectancy of only 46 years. This is 20 years below the world average, and more than 30 years below more developed regions, such as North America and Europe. Furthermore, half the population of the region was under the age of 18 in 2005. This is much higher than the world average of 34 percent, and more than double the figure for more developed regions.

Having a very young population presents two major problems. The first is that governments have to provide facilities such as education and healthcare for a very large number of children. Many countries in

A child participates in a lesson at Bweyale Primary School in Masindi, central Uganda. Although the children are receiving an education, there are still 100 pupils for every teacher, and six pupils for every textbook in this school.

the region already struggle to provide an education for all children. The second problem is that as these children will grow up and start families of their own, the population of the region will inevitably continue to grow for many years, even if the fertility rate declines.

Education for all

A basic education to at least the end of elementary school is considered a basic human right for everyone. In sub-Saharan Africa, millions of children do not enjoy this right. The United Nations Children's Fund (UNICEF) estimates that only about 57 percent of elementary school age girls and 60 percent of elementary school age boys go to school. That is lower than in any other region of the world. Education, especially for girls, is a very important factor in reducing population growth. When people have been educated they are able to read health messages, so they are more likely to make informed decisions about the timing and size of their future family. It is known that the more educated a woman is, the fewer children she is likely to have. Uganda is one country in the region to take a lead on education for all. In 1996, the government introduced universal elementary education, funding up to four children from every family to go to school. The number of children in elementary school more than doubled in a year. In Uganda today, 80 percent of primary age children go to school, which is higher than the world average! Many other countries in sub-Saharan Africa are now trying to copy the Ugandan experience.

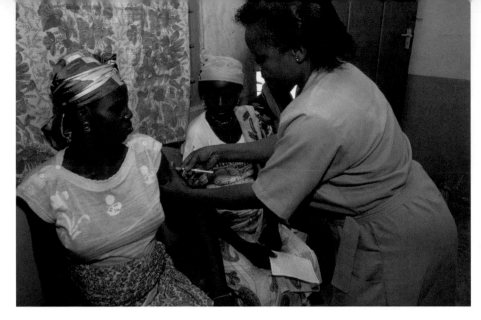

This woman in northern Ghana is being vaccinated as part of an immunization program.

Health and well-being

Poor health is one of the major obstacles to development in sub-Saharan Africa. Many of the most serious health problems could easily be avoided, however. These include diseases, such as measles and polio, which in more developed regions of the world have been brought under control by childhood immunization programs. In sub-Saharan Africa only about half of all children are currently immunized. Roughly 450,000 children a year still die from measles.

Other diseases, such as diarrhea and cholera, are related to a lack of basic facilities, such as clean water and proper toilets. Less than 60 percent of people in sub-Saharan Africa have access to a safe supply of drinking water, and less than 40 percent have access to proper toilets and sanitary conditions. Improving these basic services would save hundreds of thousands of lives.

One of the biggest diseases in sub-Saharan Africa is malaria. Malaria is caused by a parasite passed to humans through the bite of a mosquito, and kills roughly 1 million people per year. It accounts for roughly 10 percent of all disease in sub-Saharan Africa, and about 40 percent of government spending on health. The disease is thought to cost sub-Saharan Africa over $12 billion per year in lost income from those affected.

HIV and AIDS

HIV (human immunodeficiency virus) causes one of the world's most infectious diseases and has no known cure. It is transmitted through unprotected sexual contact with an infected person, or through infected blood. It can also be passed by breastfeeding mothers to their children. In time, the infected person develops AIDS (acquired immune deficiency syndrome), a condition in which their body can no longer fight off infections. In 2006, an estimated 40 million people worldwide were infected with HIV. Roughly 70 percent of that total—some 28 million cases—were in sub-Saharan Africa. Rates of infection are at 15–20 percent of the population in Southern African countries such as Botswana, Zambia, Zimbabwe, and South Africa.

HIV and AIDS are having a terrible impact across sub-Saharan Africa, affecting the economy and family life. In Zimbabwe and Botswana, for example, life expectancy has fallen from 55 years in 1970 to less than 37 years today, almost entirely due to deaths from AIDS. The most common victims are people of working age (around 18–45), so when they get sick or die this has a major impact on the economy. Another major result is the high number of children who have lost one or both of their parents. In 2006, sub-Saharan Africa had at least 12 million orphans as a result of AIDS—more than the entire child population of the United Kingdom.

Educating people about how HIV is transmitted is the most effective way to prevent the spread of the disease. Uganda's education program has been a great success—it is the only country in the region where the rate of new infections is actually falling. Medicines to keep people who are infected with HIV healthier for longer are available, but they are very expensive and still offer no cure. Many governments say they cannot afford to provide this medicine for all those who are infected.

← This poster in Sierra Leone is intended to spread the message about HIV and AIDS. Education is vital to efforts to control the spread of the disease.

Settlements and housing

The majority of people in sub-Saharan Africa still live in rural areas, and the region is one of the least urbanized in the world. In 2005, only 36 percent of the population lived in towns and cities, compared to 49 percent globally and 77 percent in the more developed regions. Urbanization levels vary greatly across the region, however. In Burundi it is 10 percent, while in Cape Verde and South Africa it is 57 percent, and in Gabon 85 percent. Urban populations are also growing faster in sub-Saharan Africa than anywhere else in the world. The growth rate for the period 1990–2004 was 4.3 percent per year—double the global average. At this rate, over half the regions' people will live in urban areas by 2030.

Ten largest cities in sub-Saharan Africa in 2005

City	Country	Population in millions
Lagos	Nigeria	10.9
Kinshasa	Democratic Republic of the Congo	6.0
Khartoum	Sudan	4.5
Abidjan	Ivory Coast	3.6
Johannesburg	South Africa	3.3
Cape Town	South Africa	3.1
East Rand (Ekurhuleni)	South Africa	3.0
Kano	Nigeria	3.0
Addis Ababa	Ethiopia	2.9
Nairobi	Kenya	2.8

Rapid urbanization brings problems. A chronic shortage of housing means people are forced to build poor quality, makeshift housing on unoccupied pieces of land. These slums, or **shanty towns** as they are called, normally lack clean water and sewers. Poor health and crime are major problems, and the risks of major disease outbreaks or disasters such as fire are much greater because of the overcrowding. The United Nations estimates that 72 percent of all city dwellers in sub-Saharan Africa live in these slums. The largest in the region is Kibera on the edge of Nairobi, Kenya, where over 1 million people live in an area of just 1 square mile (2.5 square kilometers).

Governments in some countries are attempting to address this problem. In South Africa, the government launched a reconstruction

and development program (RDP) in 1994. One of its main goals was to improve living conditions for people in urban slums. By 2004, more than 1.6 million low-cost homes had been built, and more than 9 million people had been given access to clean water. Waste collection services and electricity were also introduced into many former slums. Despite this progress, South Africa still has a major housing shortage, with an estimated 2 million homes still needed.

Slums in the Johannesburg shanty town of Alexandra. Located near the wealthy suburb of Sandton, Alexandra is one of the poorest urban areas in South Africa.

Population mobility

The main movement of people in sub-Saharan Africa takes place within national borders, and is from rural to urban areas. **Migration** across the region is less common, but does occur. Sometimes people move in search of jobs, but in many other cases they are refugees from conflict or environmental problems such as drought. Uganda, for example, has many immigrants who fled conflicts in Sudan and the Democratic Republic of the Congo.

These new homes and the electricity were part of a reconstruction and development program in South Africa in 1999.

Religion and beliefs

The people of sub-Saharan Africa follow many different religious or belief systems. Traditional belief systems based around the spirits of ancestors and the natural environment were historically the main form of religion in the region. In some countries, including Ghana, Liberia, Madagascar, Mozambique, and Togo, these are still the main belief systems today. In most countries, however, traditional beliefs have been replaced by either Christianity or Islam.

TRADITIONAL BELIEFS

It is difficult to measure how many people follow traditional beliefs, because they do not have the patterns of other religions, such as a regular day of worship, or written documents. Their beliefs and rituals are passed down by the elders. In reality, many people in sub-Saharan Africa mix traditional beliefs with mainstream religions such as Christianity or Islam. People looking for good work with a new job, for example, may pray in the mosque or church, but also visit a traditional spirit diviner or make a sacrifice to their ancestors.

Christianity

The earliest forms of Christianity in sub-Saharan Africa can be traced to Ethiopia. An early Ethiopian Church was formed there during the 4th century. The Ethiopian Church was (and still is) linked to the **Coptic Church** of Egypt, and its followers are often called Coptic Christians. Ethiopia still has the largest population of Coptic Christians anywhere in the world, accounting for roughly two-thirds of the total.

Elsewhere in sub-Saharan Africa, Christianity was introduced by European missionaries in the 19th century. They came to spread their beliefs and values to the people of Africa, but they also brought medical knowledge and education. Mission-run schools and hospitals are still found in the region today. Christianity is the most common religion in the region, but is split into many different groups. Some of the most popular and fastest-growing are the modern, **evangelical** African churches, which teach salvation through the personal acceptance of Jesus. These occasionally accommodate elements of African culture, such as polygamy (having more than one wife).

Islam

Traders from North Africa and the Middle East brought Islam to sub-Saharan Africa, from about the 5th century. Mombasa on Kenya's East

These children are studying the Koran at a Muslim school in Ibadan, Nigeria.

African coast still has a distinctly Islamic presence, because it was an important port on a trade route from the Arabian **peninsula**. Islam was more tolerant than Christianity of African cultural traditions such as polygamy, and spread rapidly. Today it is the dominant religion in the northern areas of West Africa, and is also strong in East Africa.

Sharia Law

Nigeria has long been divided between a mainly Christian south and an Islamic north. This religious difference has often been used as an excuse for conflict and violence between political and ethnic groups in the north and south. In January 2000, Zamfara state became the first of 12 states in northern Nigeria to adopt strict **Sharia laws**, in common with many Islamic states in the Middle East. Sharia laws follow the teachings of Islam and deliver strict punishments for those who do not obey. Some think these laws are too extreme. In Zamfara, for example, all businesses must close during the five periods of daily prayer observed by Muslims. The introduction of Sharia law has led to protests from Christians living in and beyond northern Nigeria. These have occasionally ended in violence. In November 2002, a Muslim protest against Nigeria hosting the Miss World beauty contest led to violence in the northern city of Kaduna in which 200 people died.

Government and stability

Since gaining independence from their colonial rulers, many countries in the region have struggled to maintain peace and stability. This is partly because their borders did not coincide with the natural groupings of people, by either language or ethnic group. These different peoples suddenly found themselves living together, but with different values, ideas, even languages. The new governments also lacked experience and were often dominated by just one ethnic group, creating jealousy and resentment from others.

Across sub-Saharan Africa, governments were overthrown by force, often by the military. Some leaders ruled with great authority in order to hold on to power, often using the army to support them. People were often denied the right to vote, and anyone opposed to the government risked being imprisoned or killed. Nigeria, for example, has had 29 years under the leadership of military **dictators** since gaining independence from the United Kingdom in 1960. In 1995 a Nigerian writer, Ken Saro-Wiwa, and eight others were executed, despite international protests, for criticizing the government and speaking out about damage being caused by the oil industry to lands controlled by the Ogoni ethnic group. Much of Nigeria's oil wealth is located in the Ogoni lands, but they have benefited little from it and the damage caused to the environment threatens their traditional way of life.

These people are voting in Sierra Leone in free presidential elections in 1996, following years of civil war and dictatorship.

THE AFRICAN UNION AND DARFUR

The **African Union** (AU) was formed in 2002 as a union of 53 African nations to promote peace, stability, cooperation, and economic growth in Africa. The AU has tried to bring lasting peace to sub-Saharan Africa, especially in the recent Darfur conflict. Roughly 7,000 AU troops have been sent to Darfur to protect people from the fighting, but this is too few for a region that is larger than France. In May 2006, the AU helped the government and rebel groups in Sudan to reach a peace agreement, but this was short-lived, and fighting continues.

Despite the problems in Darfur, the AU is developing strong cultural, economic, and political links between the countries of sub-Saharan Africa. It is hoped that closer ties will make the region more stable and reduce the chances of more conflicts.

These soldiers from Burkina Faso are on peacekeeping duty in Liberia, in 1997. They are part of an Economic Community of West Africa Monitoring Group. →

Troubled region

Sub-Saharan Africa is much more peaceful today, and most countries have democratic systems in which people vote for their government. This is not true everywhere, however. In Zimbabwe, President Robert Mugabe has been in power since 1980. During the most recent elections, he was accused of using the police and military to scare opposition supporters away from voting.

Conflicts elsewhere in the region threaten to destabilize the region as a whole. One of the most serious is in the Darfur region of Sudan. The people of Darfur say their needs are being ignored by the government in Khartoum because, unlike many of those in positions of power in Sudan, they are black Africans rather than Arabic. They also accuse the government and their supporters of trying to drive them off their land. The government denies this. In 2003, rebels in Darfur began to attack government targets. The government responded by bombing villages thought to shelter rebels. An armed **militia** called the *Janjaweed*, said to be acting for the government, attacked settlements in Darfur. More than 2 million people have had to flee their homes. By September 2006, more than 200,000 people had died as a result of the conflict.

Culture

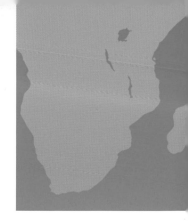

Many people talk of sub-Saharan Africa and its people as though they are all one and the same. In reality, they are no more the same than in the United Kingdom and Italy in Europe, or India and Japan in Asia. In fact there is greater diversity in Africa south of the Sahara than in almost any other region of the world. A simple example of this diversity is in the languages of the region. Sub-Saharan Africa is home to roughly 2,000 languages—one-third of the world total! It is impossible to speak of a single African culture when describing sub-Saharan Africa, but despite this the peoples of the region do share some cultural values. These include a strong sense of family, for example, with extended families and clans that can have hundreds of members. Elders are also held in very high regard in almost all African cultures. Before modern education systems were introduced, the elders of a community were the main source of the knowledge and wisdom to be passed on to future generations.

Some experts believe that sub-Saharan Africa is now facing a culture crisis. Many of its traditions, and even its languages, are being lost. This is because of greater contact with other regions of the world, particularly Western cultures. Younger generations are less interested in their own traditions and language, and more interested in the latest Western fashions or music. Other people are more optimistic. They see many new opportunities for local cultures and traditions to mix with those from other parts of the world, both within and beyond the region.

← A woman pounds spices in the village of Tiébélé, Burkina Faso. This is where the Gourounsi people live, who are famous for their architecture and decorated houses. As they paint the houses, the women sing beautiful songs together.

African languages

Language experts estimate that there are roughly 2,000 living languages (those spoken by at least one person as their main language) in sub-Saharan Africa. Nigeria alone is estimated to have 516 languages, and Cameroon 280. This makes sub-Saharan Africa one of the most language-diverse regions of the world, with 15 of the 20 most language-diverse countries. English and French are the most widely spoken languages, and have become the main languages of business and politics. They are also a common language for people to share when they do not speak each other's language. Other common languages used in this way include Arabic, Portuguese, and Swahili. English, French, and Portuguese were

← On any one day you may hear 20 or more languages being spoken in this central taxi cab station in Kampala, Uganda. Capital cities such as Kampala bring languages and cultures together.

Leading African languages spoken in the region

Language	Number of speakers (approximate in millions)	Selected countries where spoken
Swahili	48	Tanzania, Kenya, Uganda, Democratic Republic of Congo
Hausa	38	Nigeria, Niger, Togo, Cameroon, Ghana
Igbo	21	Nigeria, Cameroon
Amharic	20	Ethiopia
Yoruba	20	Nigeria, Togo, Benin, Ghana
Fula	13	Mali, Nigeria, Niger, Senegal, Sierra Leone, Togo, Benin, Burkina Faso, Chad

LANGUAGE FAMILIES

There are similarities in African languages that allow them to be grouped into four major families. The largest is the Niger-Congo family of languages. These are spoken everywhere except for the northeast part of the region. Afro-Asiatic languages are the next largest group, spoken in the north of the region and in North Africa. Nilo-Saharan languages are spoken in the northeast of the region, in countries including Uganda, Kenya, Chad, and Sudan. The smallest family is the Khoisan languages of southern Africa. Madagascar, off the east coast of southern Africa, has languages with more in common with those of Indonesia and Australia. These are known as Austronesian languages.

This map shows the distribution of the main language groups in the region.

introduced as European languages during the colonial period, and are not traditionally African.

Language barriers

Many of the languages in sub-Saharan Africa are oral languages only, meaning they have not been written down. Oral traditions such as storytelling, drama, and song have always been important in keeping these languages alive, and they remain a strong feature of many African cultures today. There are also many different **dialects** of each language, perhaps as many as 8,000 dialects across this region. A dialect is a slight variation of a language, normally confined to a specific area. This wide range of dialects can mean that people with the same language are unable to understand each other.

Language barriers can make managing issues such as education and health problematic. Few governments can afford to produce public information in every language. Language barriers can also create problems for business. To solve this, most countries in the region have adopted one or two languages as national languages, to be used for government and public use, in schools and hospitals for example, and by the business community.

Music

Despite the great cultural diversity of the region, one thing virtually all its cultures share is music. Music has long been part of daily life. Many vocal harmonies and rhythms, for example, developed out of work songs, when people sang to pass their time in the fields. Drumming is another common element of much African music, though the style and sound of drums varies greatly. In Central Africa, large drums carved from rain forest trees were once used to communicate in the dense forests. In fishing communities, fish skins were sometimes used instead of animal hides, creating a much higher-pitched drum.

← Traditional music festivals, like this one in Nairobi, Kenya, keep traditions alive and relevant by fusing them with modern styles. These are Nubian Sudanese musicians.

Modern influences

When slaves were taken from Africa to the Americas they took their musical traditions with them. Blues and jazz music developed in the southern United States as a result of this, and went on to influence modern music from rock and roll to pop and rap. Today these modern music styles are flowing back to sub-Saharan Africa, where they mix with traditional sounds to create even more new styles, such as the thriving African pop scene centered on the Democratic Republic of Congo.

There has been growing global interest in African music since the 1980s. Some artists have become internationally famous, such as Youssou N'Dour and Baaba Maal from Senegal, Fela Kuti from Nigeria, and Ladysmith Black Mambazo from South Africa. The blues guitarist Ali Farka Toure from Mali, and the jazz greats Hugh Masekela, Miriam Makeba, and Abdullah Ibrahim from South Africa, have also gained international fame.

Sports

Sports have a growing following, with soccer by far the most popular spectator sport. Many of the region's best soccer players play for European clubs, where they are among the highest paid players in the world. They return home to play for their countries in international competitions such as the Africa Nations Cup or the World Cup. Nigeria, Cameroon, and Ivory Coast are ranked among the top 20 teams in the world. In 2010, sub-Saharan Africa will see its biggest celebration of soccer yet, when South Africa hosts the World Cup—the first African nation ever to do so.

Sub-Saharan Africa is also home to some of the world's leading athletes, especially long distance runners. Kenyan runners have dominated marathon running for many years. Haile Gebrselassie from Ethiopia is one of the most successful long-distance athletes the world has known, over 5,000 and 10,000 meters. He won two Olympic gold medals (1996 and 2000) and four World Championship gold medals (1993, 1995, 1997, and 1999), and broke more than 15 world records. In women's running, nine of the top ten long distance runners in 2006 were from Ethiopia or Kenya. Athletes from these countries are acclimated to high altitude, where the air is thinner and there is less oxygen. This makes the body work harder, building strength and stamina.

These South African children are playing soccer.

Celebrations and food

Food is often the focus of ceremonies and festivals in the region. Weddings and funerals can involve elaborate traditional feasts lasting several days. One famous food-related festival is Iwa-ji, the yam festival of the Igbo people, who live mainly in southern Nigeria. Iwa-ji takes place in August and involves the performance of traditional ceremonies to give thanks for the harvest, as well as dancing, drama, and feasting. Other cultures follow similar harvest celebrations, such as Inkwala (Festival of the First Fruits), which takes place in Swaziland in December or January.

Diets

The diets of people in sub-Saharan Africa vary according to their environment. Around the shores of Lake Victoria, for example, various forms of banana are a **staple**, benefiting from the regular rainfall in the area. In drier regions, common crops include millet, sorghum, and cassava. Corn is widely grown in southern and eastern Africa. Corn flour is used to make a porridge or doughy paste. Rice is another staple in parts of West and East Africa, but needs a plentiful supply of water to grow. Staple foods are normally eaten with a sauce made from vegetables (onions, tomatoes, beans, and greens are among the most common) or meat. In coastal, lakeside, and river communities, fish is often used to make sauces.

Nutrition and health

Although staple crops are filling, they are not very nutritious. Those with plenty of land or a reasonable income can make up for this by growing or buying other foods. But for many of the poorest people, providing a varied, healthy diet can be very difficult. As a result, **malnutrition** is a major problem in sub-Saharan Africa.

The worst form of malnutrition is hunger, where people cannot get enough energy from food to work. If they cannot farm the land, it is even harder for them to get enough food. In 2006, it was estimated that at least 35 million people in Africa, almost all of them in sub-Saharan Africa, were suffering from hunger. Some of the worst affected countries include Sudan, Ethiopia, Somalia, Malawi, Mozambique, Zimbabwe, and Niger, all of which have experienced recent droughts that made the problem worse. Food aid from other parts of the country or from international agencies can help in the short term, but longer term solutions are needed. These include improving basic healthcare, so that people are stronger to resist periods of hunger, and improving people's rights to the land so that they can grow what they need. Malnutrition and poor health cannot be separated from poverty, and so helping people out of poverty must be the priority.

A Somali woman breaks up corn cobs that will be ground into a flour for use in cooking. Corn is an important staple crop in the region, but has little nutritional value.

Natural Resources and Economy

Sub-Saharan Africa is the poorest region in the world. Over time it has become even poorer compared with the rest of the world. In 1990, the World Bank calculated that the average income per person there was about 15 percent that of the world average. By 2005, this had fallen to just 10 percent. The poverty of the region is even more obvious when individual countries are compared. In 1971, average incomes in the United States were roughly 28 times higher than incomes in Nigeria, but by 2005 they were almost 78 times higher. Over the same time period, average incomes in the United Kingdom, for example, increased from 15 to 71 times higher than incomes in Kenya. Even though incomes have increased, they are not keeping pace with the rest of the world.

Wealth is very unevenly distributed across the region. South Africa is responsible for roughly 40 percent of the entire region's income; average incomes here are almost seven times the regional average. Within countries, too, there are big differences in wealth. In fact there are few other regions of the world with such inequalities in wealth. They are shown in people's quality of life including education, healthcare, and housing.

One of the main challenges for sub-Saharan Africa is to improve its economies and enjoy a greater share of global wealth. Ever since the colonial period, it has depended on a few key exports (mainly minerals or agricultural goods) for nearly all of its income. Higher earning industries, such as manufacturing and services, are poorly developed.

← These Zulu women on the highway in Durban, South Africa, sell roots, herbs, and plants used for medicine and magic. In the distance is the city's business district.

In Zimbabwe, a woman is carefully fertilizing her corn plants. Subsistence farming like this is very labor intensive. Much of the work is done by women.

Subsistence farming

This is one of the few regions of the world where **subsistence farming** is still a dominant economic activity. In subsistence farming, people produce food mainly for their own use, and sell only a small surplus locally to earn money for other needs. This is how many people are employed in the region. In Burkina Faso, Tanzania, and Sudan, for example, more than 80 percent of the population is involved in small-scale subsistence farming.

Cash crops

Cash crops are grown purely for sale, and the farmers use the income from selling them to buy their own food and other goods. The main cash crops in Africa are cotton, tea, coffee, sugar, cocoa, and tobacco. Cash crop farmers normally sell their produce to factories or export companies, who process them and sell them on around the world. The farmer gets only a basic price for the crop, most of the profit is made by the factories and exporters.

Cash crops are also grown by **plantation** or commercial farms. Many of these were set up during the colonial period by Europeans, who took over the best farmland and employed local people to grow cash crops to export back to Europe. The area of Kericho in Kenya, for example, is dominated by the tea industry. Large, European-owned tea plantations employ tens of thousands of people to pick and process the tea, ready for export. In this way Europe continues to earn large profits by growing cash crops in sub-Saharan Africa.

Falling prices, unfair trade

One problem facing agriculture in sub-Saharan Africa is that the price of many commodities (goods) has been falling for decades. Between 1980 and 2000, the world price of coffee fell by 64 percent, cocoa by 71 percent and sugar by 77 percent. This means that every year farmers must grow more to earn the same amount—but in growing more they increase the supply, so prices fall further. When there is a high supply of something its price normally falls, and when supply is low it rises.

Another problem is that the region's farmers cannot compete with farmers in Europe and North America, where governments support farmers with payments called **subsidies**. In the United States, for example, cotton farmers are paid roughly twice the real market value of their cotton. Farmers in West Africa can produce cotton much more cheaply than farmers in the United States, but they receive a low price for it because of overproduction by U.S. cotton farmers. Wealthier nations also impose high taxes on the price of agricultural goods they import from Africa and elsewhere, to protect their own farmers. These make goods grown in sub-Saharan Africa more expensive and harder for African farmers to sell.

HORTICULTURE

A new, higher-value type of agriculture called **horticulture** is expanding rapidly in sub-Saharan Africa. This involves farmers growing fruit, spices, nuts, vegetables, and flowers for export to wealthy nations. In countries such as Ghana, Kenya, Tanzania, Zambia, and South Africa, horticulture is becoming an important industry. Horticulture uses expensive technology, such as computer-controlled watering systems, so it is mostly done by large, plantation-type farms rather than by small-scale farmers.

These workers are harvesting grapes at a winery near Cape Town, South Africa, in a large-scale operation.

Resource rich

Sub-Saharan Africa is rich in natural resources. It has timber, coal, oil, gold, diamonds, and precious metals. The problem is that they are not evenly distributed, so only a few countries benefit from them. They are also normally controlled by just a few people or companies, and these are often from abroad. Many of the profits never benefit the local people.

Leading natural resources by country, 2004-05

Resource	Country	Share of world production (percent)	World rank
Diamonds	Botswana	19.7	2
Gold	South Africa	13.5	1
Cobalt	Congo DR	33	1
Platinum	South Africa	58	1
Uranium	Namibia	8.1	4
Coal	South Africa	4.8	5
Oil	Nigeria	3.2	12

Energy resources

Most energy resources in the region are in Nigeria and South Africa. Nigeria is rich in oil. In 2005, it accounted for 3 percent of the world's known oil reserves, and 3.2 percent of world oil production. Angola, Cameroon, Equatorial Guinea, Sudan, Chad, Gabon, and the Congo also produce oil. Of these, only Angola with 1.6 percent of world production is anywhere near as important as Nigeria. The oil wealth of Nigeria has been a cause of great dispute, as the people whose land the oil is on say they do not benefit from it. They also suffer from pollution, as people steal oil from the pipelines that run across their land. Coal is the main energy resource in South Africa.

↑ People row a boat next to pipelines to the coast terminal run by the Nigerian National Petroleum Company (NNPC). The pipelines show evidence of oil leaks and oil fires.

Non-energy resources

Sub-Saharan Africa has many non-energy resources, and is among the world's leading producers of important minerals. In 2004, for instance, the region produced 60 percent of the world's platinum ore, 55 percent of its diamonds, 47 percent of its cobalt, 22 percent of its gold, and nearly 18 percent of its uranium. Like energy resources, these tend to be concentrated in just a few countries. South Africa has the greatest mineral wealth overall, and the broadest range of minerals. Other countries are rich in one or two key minerals, such as uranium in Niger and cobalt and copper in Zambia. Chad and Malawi have virtually no non-energy minerals.

Conflict diamonds

Diamonds have been at the center of a major controversy in some sub-Saharan African countries, where they are being used to fund wars and international terrorism. Sierra Leone is one such country. A rebel army called the Revolutionary United Front (RUF) took control of diamond producing areas in Sierra Leone in the early 1990s. They forced mine workers to work in appalling conditions, and created an army (including child soldiers) to protect the mines. The diamonds were sold to Europe, North America, and other wealthy regions. In the late 1990s, European diamond traders were buying $125 million worth of diamonds a year from the RUF. New regulations on the international trade in diamonds were introduced in 2003, but the illegal trade in conflict diamonds continues. In Sierra Leone, the conflict diamond trade is believed to have killed up to 70,000 people and severely injured more than 20,000 since 1991.

← Working conditions are appalling in this diamond mine in the Moa River, Sierra Leone.

Service industries

Service industries such as banking, insurance, communications, transportation, and tourism have not historically been well developed in the region, but this is changing fast, thanks to new technology such as the Internet and mobile phones. It is now possible, for example, to use the Internet to book a vacation directly with a company based in the region. Mobile phones have also opened up many new business opportunities. In Uganda they are being used to call bicycle taxis (called *boda bodas*), creating a boom in this cheap and local form of transportation. Mobile phones are also improving other services, from mobile hairdressers to mobile health workers.

More than 75 percent of all telephones in sub-Saharan Africa are mobile phones. The number of subscribers increased from 0.02 per 1,000 people in 1990 to 74.8 per 1,000 by 2004. South Africa has the highest proportion of mobile phone subscribers, and the most developed service sector. Many international companies have offices here, and the Johannesburg stock exchange is one of the most important in the world.

Tourism

One of the few major service industries in sub-Saharan Africa is tourism. In 2004, tourism produced roughly 12 percent of all export earnings in the region overall. Tourism is even more important in the Seychelles and Cape Verde Islands. Millions of people travel to the region every year on safari vacations, to see the wildlife, and to experience the region's beaches and different cultures.

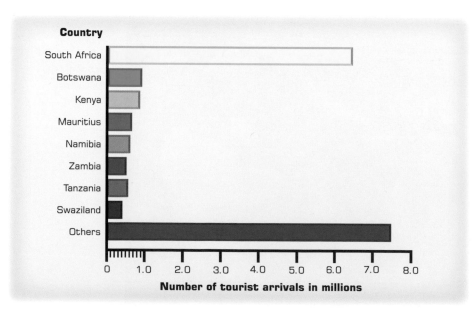

← This bar chart shows the number of international tourist arrivals in 2004 in the top eight countries in the region, plus the combined figure for the remaining countries.

Brain drain

Many of the best teachers, health professionals, engineers, and scientists in the region are leaving to find higher-paid jobs in wealthier regions such as North America or Europe. There are more African engineers and scientists working in the United States than there are in Africa, for example. Many wealthier countries actively recruit these professionals to solve their own labor shortages. This problem is known as a brain drain. The shortage of key professionals affects the quality of services available for local people. Only 42 percent of births in sub-Saharan Africa are attended by trained health professionals, for example, compared to 99 percent in the United States, the United Kingdom, and Australia. The ratio of doctors to patients is another good indicator of the problem. In the United States, the United Kingdom, or Australia there is about one doctor for every 425 people. In South Africa there is one doctor for every 1,300 people, and in Malawi, Niger, and Togo there is only one doctor for every 25,000 people. Wealthier nations within the region also create a brain drain. South Africa and Namibia attract professionals from poorer parts of the region.

Adventure activities, including rafting, trekking, and overland expeditions, are attracting more new tourists to the region. These tourists are on safari to see the animals in the Maasai Mara Reserve, Kenya.

Sharing the benefits

Although it is one of the poorest regions of the world, there are pockets of wealth within sub-Saharan Africa, but this wealth is not shared at either a country or a regional level. In 2005, for example, the average income per person in South Africa was $4,960, 16 times the average in neighboring Mozambique. The gap between the wealthiest (Seychelles, $8,290) and poorest (Burundi, $100) was almost 83 times! Within countries, too, there are great inequalities in wealth. In Namibia, the wealthiest 20 percent of the population have almost 80 percent of the country's income. The poorest 20 percent have only 1 percent of it. This pattern is repeated across the region, with the wealthiest 20 percent having roughly 55 percent of income, and the poorest 20 percent only roughly 5 percent.

This sign in Sierra Leone encourages people to report corruption to the authorities. It is part of a government program to reduce the damage to the economy caused by corrupt practices.

CRIME AND CORRUPTION

The poverty in sub-Saharan Africa has led some people to turn to crime and corruption to improve their incomes. Large cities such as Nairobi, Lagos, Cape Town, and Kinshasa are associated with criminal gangs. The houses of the rich are surrounded by electric fences and patrolled by armed security guards. In Nairobi and Johannesburg, armed carjacking is a problem.

Corruption is not normally violent, but it is still criminal. People in positions of power demand money from others just to allow them to go about their daily business. In Nigeria, for example, police officers set up roadblocks and demand money from people to continue on their journey. These bribes are normally small, but across the region they add up to millions of dollars every year.

One way to better spread this wealth is through more trade, but Africa's share in world trade is falling. In 1980 it was roughly 6 percent, today it is just 2 percent. Within Africa, only 12 percent of goods go to other African countries. Increasing trade within sub-Saharan Africa could spread wealth there by creating a demand for local goods and services.

Black market

Trade is made more difficult by often slow and complicated paperwork. Many officials also demand bribes in return for the right papers. One reaction to this is a large **black market**, or unofficial economy. This is when people run businesses without paying taxes or keeping records. They provide affordable goods and services for the millions of people in the region living in poverty. In cities such as Nairobi in Kenya, or Cape Town in South Africa, it is estimated that the black market may account for up to 80 percent of economic activity. The black market is a problem for governments, because they are not collecting taxes from those businesses. Without the black market, however, the local economy might collapse. In Uganda, Kenya, and other countries, governments are working to reduce the barriers to trade and to stop corruption, in order to encourage more businesses to be part of the official economy and pay their taxes, which can then be used to improve services such as healthcare and education.

← This gasoline vendor in Chad's capital, N'djamena, is part of the black market. Many traders sell gasoline smuggled from Nigeria, offering it more cheaply than at legitimate gas stations.

Poverty and debt

Even the wealthiest nations in sub-Saharan Africa are poor compared with countries in North America or Europe. Poverty remains the biggest challenge for the region, with roughly 45 percent of its people living on less than $1 per day—the cost of a typical soft drink in the United States. If the daily living amount for measuring poverty is increased to $2 per day, 75 percent of people in the region are living in poverty. In Nigeria, Tanzania, and Zambia this increases to more than 90 percent.

One of the biggest barriers many sub-Saharan African countries face in reducing poverty is debt. When these countries became independent, they were given large amounts of money by wealthier countries as loans, to help them develop. They would build roads, provide energy, improve agriculture, and increase trade, so their economies could grow and they could repay the loans. But these economies have not grown, and much of the money was never spent as it should have been. Corrupt leaders used the money for their own benefit. Now, many countries in the region have enormous debts equivalent to one-third or more of their national income. In The Gambia, debts are equivalent to 105 percent of income, and in recently war-torn Liberia debts have reached more than 760 percent of national income!

Drop the debt

Countries cannot invest in their economies, and the well-being of their own people, because they are trying to repay these debts. In the 1990s, a campaign to drop the debts of sub-Saharan African countries gained international support. It argued that the money should be spent locally on development projects instead. In 1996, many wealthy nations agreed to reduce or cancel debts to the poorest countries, but progress has been slow. This is because the countries must first meet strict conditions to make sure the money is used properly for the benefit of all, not the corrupt few. Protesters argue that this delay is costing lives, as poverty continues to kill thousands of people every day. Uganda was one of the first countries to have its debt canceled, and the money released has delivered clean water to an additional 2.2 million people. Each delay also means a growing debt. In 1970, the debts of sub-Saharan Africa were roughly $6.9 billion. Today they total roughly $235 billion.

Unlocking the potential

Sub-Saharan Africa is a region of great potential, but historical patterns of colonialism and unfair trade keep much of this potential locked up. Farmers cannot compete with those in North America or Europe who are paid subsidies by their governments. Businesses cannot sell their goods because expensive taxes prevent them from exporting to wealthy nations. Removing these obstacles would allow sub-Saharan Africa to compete more equally in the global trading system, and enjoy a greater share of the world's wealth. Reducing the debts and poverty of the region would help the countries to invest in an educated workforce to meet these new opportunities, and might stop the loss of skilled Africans to other parts of the world. The African Union recognizes the need to face these challenges as a region, and for individual countries to support each other through closer political and economic ties. This is a positive first move, but for the true potential of the region to emerge, the rest of the world must also give sub-Saharan Africa a chance.

← Sub-Saharan Africa needs support to unlock its potential. Here a leading aid administrator is being shown an aid project to develop science, mathematics, and technology skills in Alexandra township, South Africa. The rejuvenation of Alexandra involves community organizations and private business as well as local and national governments and international aid.

Fact File

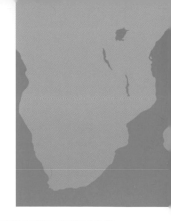

Country	Population	Area in sq miles (sq km)	Capital city
Angola	15,941,392	481,226 (1,246,700)	Luanda
Benin	8,438,853	112,620 (433,331)	Porto-Novo
Botswana	1,764,926	231,742 (600,370)	Gaborone
Burkina Faso	13,227,835	105,841 (274,200)	Ouagadougou
Burundi	7,547,515	10,742 (27,830)	Bujumbura
Cameroon	16,321,863	183,519 (475,440)	Yaounde
Cape Verde	506,807	1,556 (4,033)	Praia
Central African Republic	4,037,747	240,471 (622,984)	Bangui
Chad	9,748,931	495,755 (1,284,000)	N'Djamena
Comoros	600,490	837 (2,170)	Moroni
Congo, Dem. Republic	57,548,744	905,328 (2,345,410)	Kinshasa
Congo, Republic	3,998,904	132,012 (342,000)	Brazzaville
Cote d'Ivoire	18,153,868	124,469 (322,460)	Yamoussoukro
Djibouti	793,078	8,878 (23,000)	Djibouti
Equatorial Guinea	503,519	10,827 (28,051)	Malabo
Eritrea	4,401,357	46,829 (121,320)	Asmara
Ethiopia	71,256,000	435,071 (1,127,127)	Addis Ababa
Gabon	1,383,841	103,319 (267,667)	Libreville
Gambia, The	1,517,079	4,361 (11,300)	Banjul
Ghana	22,112,804	92,431 (239,460)	Accra
Guinea	9,402,098	94,900 (245,857)	Conakry
Guinea-Bissau	1,586,344	13,942 (36,120)	Bissau
Kenya	34,255,720	224,902 (582,650)	Nairobi
Lesotho	1,794,769	11,717 (30,355)	Maseru

Liberia	3,283,267	42,988 (111,370)	Monrovia
Madagascar	18,605,922	226,597 (587,040)	Antananarivo
Malawi	12,883,935	45,733 (118,480)	Lilongwe
Mali	13,518,416	478,640 (1,240,000)	Bamako
Mauritania	3,068,742	397,850 (1,030,700)	Nouakchott
Mauritius	1,248,000	787 (2,040)	Port Louis
Mayotte (France)	201,234	144 (374)	Mamoudzou
Mozambique	19,792,296	309,413 (801,590)	Maputo
Namibia	2,031,252	318,611 (825,418)	Windhoek
Niger	13,956,977	489,062 (1,267,000)	Niamey
Nigeria	131,529,672	356,574 (923,768)	Lagos
Rwanda	9,037,690	10,166 (26,338)	Kigali
Sao Tome and Principe	156,523	386 (1,001)	Sao Tome
Senegal	11,658,172	75,729 (196,190)	Dakar
Seychelles	84,494	175 (455)	Victoria
Sierra Leone	5,525,478	27,691 (71,740)	Freetown
Somalia	8,227,826	246,135 (637,657)	Mogadishu
South Africa	45,192,000	470,886 (1,219,912)	Pretoria
Sudan	36,232,944	967,499 (2,505,810)	Khartoum
Swaziland	1,131,000	6,702 (17,363)	Mbabane
Tanzania	38,328,808	364,803 (945,087)	Dar es Salaam
Togo	6,145,004	21,908 (56,785)	Lome
Uganda	28,816,228	91,111 (236,040)	Kampala
Zambia	11,668,457	290,509 (752,614)	Lusaka
Zimbabwe	13,009,534	150,763 (390,580)	Harare

Note: population figures are projected estimates for 2008.

Timeline

c.3 million BCE	Pre-human ancestors are living in Africa. Remains have been found dating to this period.
c.100,000 BCE	Early humans evolved in Africa and gradually spread out around the world.
c.600–1250	Early African states (kingdoms) emerge in West Africa, including those of Ghana, Mali, Hausa, and Benin.
c.1550	Portuguese traders establish trading posts around much of the African coastline. These are some of the earliest European contacts with Africa.
c.1600–1870	European powers including the British, Dutch, French, Spanish, Belgians, Germans, and Portuguese all develop trading or missionary interests in sub-Saharan Africa.
1885	A conference of European powers in Berlin carves Africa up into colonial territories. Many of the borders drawn at this time remain today.
1914	Every country in sub-Saharan Africa, except for South Africa, Ethiopia, and Liberia, is controlled by a European colonial power.
1948	The South African government introduces a policy of apartheid that divides the rights and mobility of people living in South Africa according to their race.
c.1950s	Nile perch and tilapia are introduced into Lake Victoria.
1957	Ghana gains independence from the United Kingdom, beginning a period of decolonization in Africa.
1963	The Organization of African Unity (OAU) is formed.
1981	The African Economic Community (AEC) is formed.
1984	A massive famine in Ethiopia and Sudan shocks the world and raises the profile of African issues internationally.

1990	Namibia becomes a country, independent from South Africa. Nelson Mandela, the anti-apartheid leader, is released from prison in South Africa. This signaled the gradual dismantling of apartheid.
1993	Eritrea becomes a country, independent from Ethiopia.
1994	Nelson Mandela is elected president of South Africa in the country's first free elections since the end of apartheid, when all people are allowed to vote.
1994	**Genocide** in Rwanda leads to more than 800,000 deaths.
1995	In Nigeria, writer Ken Saro-Wiwa and eight others are executed for their protests against the government.
1996	The Ugandan government introduces a universal primary education (UPE) program, to fund four children in every family through primary school.
2000	Zamfara state in Nigeria adopts Sharia laws. Other states in Nigeria follow.
2002	The African Union, comprising 53 African nations, is formed.
2003	Conflict escalates in the Darfur region of Sudan, between the government and the local population.
2005	The G8 group, the world's eight richest nations, makes Africa's poverty a priority issue.
2005	The British government releases a report from the Commission for Africa to consider the continent's future.
2006	A logging operation in Congo becomes the first in sub-Saharan Africa to be given approval by the Forestry Stewardship Council (FSC).

Glossary

African Union	union of 53 African nations, formed in 2002, as a forum for discussion and action on issues of common concern to the continent
AIDS	acquired immunodeficiency syndrome, a disease in which the body can no longer fight off infections. There is no known cure for AIDS.
alkaline	when something is alkaline it has a pH value of above 7 and is the opposite of acidic. Alkaline waters contain a high concentration of salts.
archaeologist	scientist who studies old objects and places to understand more about how people lived in the past
arid	dry, with average rainfall of 1–8 inches (25–200 millimeters) per year. Hyper-arid zones have less than 1 inch (25 millimeters) of rainfall per year. Semi-arid zones have an annual average rainfall of 8–20 inches (200–500 millimeters).
basin	area of land drained by a river or group of rivers
black market	the unofficial economy, when people run businesses without paying taxes or keeping records
cash crops	crops that are grown to sell for money. They include coffee, sugar cane, cocoa, tea, apples, and oranges.
climate	general weather conditions in an area over a long period of time
colony	territory controlled by another country and normally inhabited (colonized) by people from that country. Kenya was a colony of the United Kingdom, for example.
continent	one of Earth's seven large land masses. Africa is a continent.
Coptic Church	branch of the Christian Church originally founded in Egypt in the 6th century
desertification	condition in which soils lose their fertility. This can be due to topsoil loss because of erosion or the removal of vegetation, or as a result of intensive agriculture that fails to give soils time to recover between growth cycles.
desert or dryland	very dry region, with less than 1 inch (25 millimeters) of rainfall per year
dictator	ruler who governs harshly with unlimited power
dialect	regional variety of a language
ecosystem	the contents of an environment, including all the plants and animals that live there. This could be a pond, a forest, or the entire Earth.
erosion	wearing away of soil or rock by the wind and rain, or by people through deforestation
evangelical	Christian churches that are very active in recruiting people to share in their beliefs
genocide	the killing of a large number of people from the same racial or religious group
HIV	human immunodeficiency virus, a deadly virus spread by having unprotected sex, using contaminated needles, or receiving contaminated blood. HIV can develop into AIDS.

horticulture	growing plants such as flowers, fruits, and vegetables in gardens or greenhouses
hydroelectric power	electricity produced by moving water, especially from a dam across a river
immunization	process of giving drugs to people to protect them from known diseases. Immunization prevents millions of deaths from preventable diseases.
irrigate	to water land in order to help crops grow
life expectancy	the average number of years someone would be expected to live
malnutrition	deficiency in the nutrients which are essential for the development of the body and for keeping it healthy in adulthood
migration	movement of people (migrants) to or from an area. Migration can be regular, seasonal, or permanent.
militia	military force, often made up of civilians
missionary	someone sent to another country by their church to spread its beliefs or to carry out social work, such as teaching or medicine
nomadic	referring to a group of people (nomads) who constantly move from place to place in search of pasture for their animals
pastoralist	someone whose livelihood depends on caring for domestic animals such as cattle, goats, or sheep
peninsula	piece of land that juts out into the sea
plantation	farming system where a single crop is grown. Rubber, palm, coffee, tea, and sugar are major crops grown in this way.
population density	number of people who live in a standard area (such as a square mile or kilometer)
predator	animal that hunts or preys upon other animals
rain forest	tropical habitat in which trees form the dominant species. Regular rainfall and stable temperatures allow these trees to grow all year round.
savanna	plain covered in grassland, with few trees
service industry	industry such as banking, insurance, or transportation that provides services to other industries or the general population
shanty town	makeshift settlement close to an urban center. Shanty towns normally lack basic services and are often built illegally.
Sharia laws	laws based on the teachings of Islam and adopted by several countries where Islam is the dominant religion
staple	type of food that forms the major part of a diet. Rice, wheat, corn, bread, and potatoes are examples of staple foods.
subsidy	payment made to producers by a government to help them with the cost of production or to ensure they are paid a minimum amount for what they produce
subsistence farming	form of farming that provides food mainly for the household. A small surplus of food may be sold.
tropics	area of Earth that lies between the Tropic of Cancer in the north and the Tropic of Capricorn in the south, roughly 1,600 miles (2,575 kilometers) either side of the Equator.

Find Out More

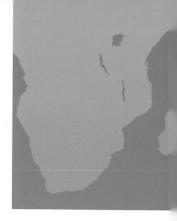

Further reading

Bowden, Rob. *Continents of the World: Africa*. London: Hodder Wayland, 2005.

Downing, David. *Troubled World: Africa—Postcolonial Conflict*.Chicago: Heinemann Library, 2004.

Oppong, Joseph. *Modern World Cultures: Africa South of the Sahara*. New York: Chelsea House, 2005.

Websites

www.africa-union.org

The website for the African Union, with information on its work and events including country profiles and maps.

www.uneca.org

This is the database of the United Nations Economic Commission for Africa, very useful for up-to-date statistics and news about the continent.

www.undp.org/africa

The Africa pages of the United Nations Development Program include key documents and news items relating to the development of the continent.

www-sul.stanford.edu/depts/ssrg/africa/guide.html

This website has links to other online materials about sub-Saharan Africa, organized by country or by topic.

www.pbs.org/wnet/africa
This website accompanies a television series in the United States that covered the major ecosystems of Africa and looked at their people and wildlife. It is very good for reference and for links.

www.lonelyplanet.com/worldguide/destinations/africa
This travel guide to individual African countries has "fast facts," featured attractions, and tourist information.

Activities

Here are some topics to research if you want to find out more about sub-Saharan Africa:

HIV/AIDS in sub-Saharan Africa
How many people are infected with HIV/AIDS? Which countries are the worst affected? What is being done about HIV/AIDS in the region? What is the impact of HIV/AIDS on the people and economies of the region? There is a lot of useful information about this important topic, but a good place to start is: www.unaids.org/en/Regions_Countries/Regions/SubSaharanAfrica.asp.

Climate change and Africa
How will a changing climate affect the people and environments of Africa south of the Sahara? Will there be more droughts or more floods? Will people be forced to move? What can be done about this? A good place to begin exploring climate change in the region is: www.oxfam.org.uk/what_we_do/issues/climate_change/africa_up_in_smoke.htm.

The history of Africa
How did religions come to Africa? How did slavery affect the region? What did the colonial period really mean? How did countries in the region become independent? There is so much to explore about the history of Africa, but a good starting points is: www.bbc.co.uk/worldservice/africa/features/storyofafrica/index.shtml.

Index